Great Songs of
MADISON AVENUE

D0470305

Great Songs of
MADISON AVENUE

Edited by
Peter and Craig Norback

Musical Arrangements and Autography by
Kenneth J. Costa

Exclusive Distributors to the Music Trade

Hal Leonard Publishing
Corporation

782. 42
GRE
c.01

Quadrangle/The New York Times Book Co.

Second printing, March 1977

Copyright©1976 by Quadrangle/The New York Times
Book Company, Inc. All rights reserved, including the
right to reproduce this book or portions thereof in any
form. For information, address: Quadrangle/ The New York
Times Book Company, Inc., Three Park Avenue, New York,
N.Y. 10016. Manufactured in the United States of
America. Published simultaneously in Canada by
Fitzhenry & Whiteside, Ltd., Toronto.

Library of Congress Card Number: 75-37374

International Standard Book Number: 0-8129-0626-8

Contents

4

Introduction

People love jingles. They love them as much as their cars, their favorite movie stars, even their hamburgers and French fries . . . perhaps more.

But eight or so months ago, before our copyist put a single note on paper, this belief was not shared by everyone; nor were our editors entirely convinced. In fact, the skeptics outnumbered the faithful 4 to 2.

Not knowing exactly how to begin such a project, we thought small and selected seven companies, a lucky number as it turned out, and sent a letter requesting permission to include their jingles in the book. We tried to use corporate words like "logo," "world rights," "proof copies for final approval," etc., things we thought would put the top executives' minds at ease.

About three weeks later we received inquisitive, yet cautious replies (corporate words are a myth), and learned that company executives loved jingles, too . . . theirs and others, it makes no difference. To say we started a minor commotion in the industry is putting it mildly. Everybody in the jingle chain of command, from the company president to the composer, became enthusiastic about the idea of a jingle songbook.

Needless to say, with a unaminous shrug of the shoulders, the skeptics converted and set us to work. So for the six months we talked and sang with hundreds of corporate executives and counselors, advertising executives and composers in our hurried endeavor to collect the GREAT SONGS OF MADISON AVENUE.

And, though the job of coordinating company, ad agency, and composer to extract words, music, logos, and permissions often entailed delicate diplomacy, there were what we liked to call "people moments." Probably the best example we have of such a moment is the postscript in the letter from the inveterate jingle-hummer, William Braznell, Jr., Manager, Public Relations, Del Monte Corporation. He closed his letter by quietly requesting, "P.S. Hope you won't fail to include my all-time favorite, 'Ajax, (boom-boom) the foaming cleanser.'" We didn't! (Page 212)

Also, in our telephone trek around the country, collecting these jingle masterpieces, we heard some very interesting and surprising stories. Out of World War II came the *Sound Off March*. Not spontaneously as one might imagine although it does seem that way considering that the song is an integral part of marching.

"Sound Off! (One, two) Oh, you Sound Off! (Three, four)."

It has played hundreds of bit parts in war films and, as many recent recruits have learned, it's the song of the military afoot.

"Sound Off! (One, two) Now you Sound Off! (Three, four)."

Actually, it became a popular song and musical score for the famous *Sound Off For Chesterfield* commercial. (Page 182)

The truth is the *Sound Off March* did start in the Army, in World War II, but was the work of a private, Willie Lee Duckworth, who wrote and then found a New York publisher for his song. It's been a financial comfort to the author and publisher ever since.

Another one of those never-to-be forgotten songs that seems to belong to the ages is *Happy Birthday To You*. The "most sung" tune (*Guinness World Book Of Records*) was the creation of two sisters, Mildred J. and Patty S. Hill, who penned and copyrighted the song in 1935. Of course, there are a number of company and ad agency executives who know this fact, but they learned it the hard way . . . after their great new jingle campaign had hit the air.

One fact we can't really verify, but one which is generally held true by the industry is that *Have You Tried Wheaties* (page 72), is the oldest jingle on record. It was first introduced in the '20s making the jingle industry over 50 years old. Obviously the tunes and the words for jingles have come a long way since then, but the Wheaties song still sounds pretty good.

We really enjoyed putting this book together; in fact, we had fun. But we couldn't have done it without a lot of help. So we'd like to thank all the people at the various companies and advertising agencies who graciously helped us hunt down jingle lead sheets and logos. Also, we'd like to express our thanks to Larry Levinson, Stan Applebaum, and Steve Kanych . . . and a very special thanks to Sid Woloshin for all his help.

Now, if you please, Maestro . . .

Craig and Peter Norback

A Scrumpdillyishus Day

Words by Robert Larranaga &
Dale Menten

Music by Dale Menten

Oh, it's a ve-ry mer-ry con-fec-tion-e-ry, scrump-dil-ly-ish-us day,

It's in-cred-i-bly ed-i-bly tan-ta-li-zing I mean it's a per-fect day,

So let's all go to the Dair-y Queen, the scrump-dil-ly-ish-us

*Reg. U.S. Pat. Off., Am. D.Q. Corp. (c) 1976 Am. D.Q. Corp.

Copyright 1973 by American Dairy Queen Corp.
All rights reserved.

10

Air France Makes It Easy To Get There

AIR FRANCE

Words by Doris Elliott
Music by Don Elliott

Copyright 1973 by Air France
Permission to reproduce granted by Air France

11

Aqua Velva Man

some-thing a- bout A-qua Vel-va, a man wants to feel like a man,

feel like a man, 'cause there's some-thing a-bout an A-qua Vel-va man.

Copyright 1974 by The J. B. Williams Company, Inc.
Permission to reproduce granted by The J. B. Williams Company, Inc.

Ask Any Mermaid

Written by Dick Marx & Associates

Moderato

Do you be-lieve in mer-maids, a lot of peo-ple do,

Please be-lieve in mer-maids, They be-lieve in you,

Just ask an-y mer-maid you hap-pen to see, What's the best tu-na?

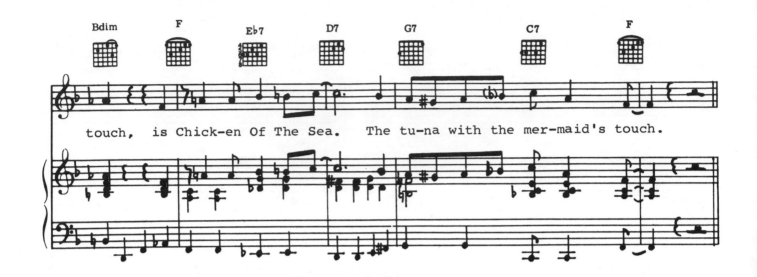

touch, is Chick-en Of The Sea. The tu-na with the mer-maid's touch.

Copyright 1970 by Ralston Purina Company

16

Aunt Jemima
(Silver Dollar)

Written by Jack Palmer &
Clarke Van Ness

TRO - © Copyright 1939 (renewed 1967) and 1950 by Essex Music, Inc., New York, N.Y.

Aunt Jemima

Bit-O-Honey

Rock beat

Written by Ben Allen

I took a lit—tle bit of mon—ey, And then I bought a Bit O'

Hon—ey, 'Cuz ev—'ry bit o' Bit-O-Honey® Goes a long, long

way. Six big piec—es in ev—'ry bar, And

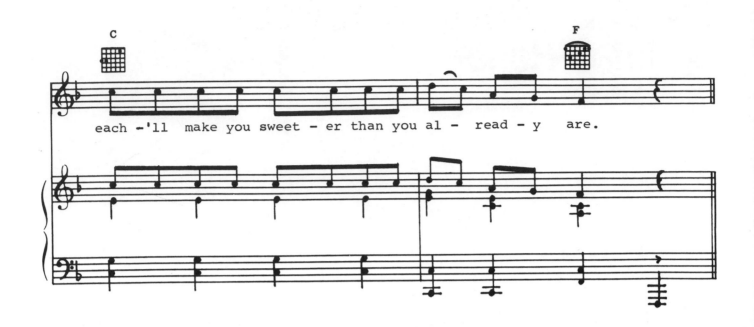

each –'ll make you sweet - er than you al - read - y are.

BIT·O·HONEY®

Copyright 1966 by Ward-Johnston, Inc.

Bringing Up Baby

Moderato

If there's a ba-by in your house, be it a Lord or

La-dy, then hark to what the Ger-ber folks say, on bring-ing up your

ba-by. Now here's an-oth-er Ger-ber thought that's sure to please your

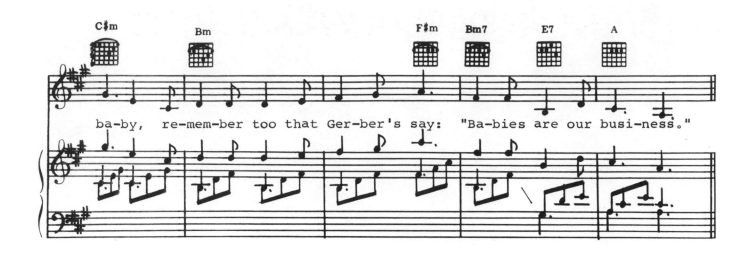

ba-by, re-mem-ber too that Ger-ber's say: "Ba-bies are our busi-ness."

Gerber®

Copyright 1954, 1956, 1957, 1958, 1961 & 1963 by Gerber Products Company

Brush Your Teeth With Colgate

Written by Robert Forshaw

Moderato

Brush your teeth with Col-gate, Col-gate Den-tal Cream, it cleans your breath (what a tooth-paste), while it guards your teeth.

Permission to reproduce granted by Colgate-Palmolive Company

Brylcreem, A Little Dab'll Do Ya

Written by John P. Atherton

Brylcreem

Permission to reproduce words granted by Beecham Products.
Copyright 1949 by Atherton & Currier, Inc.

Buster Brown Shoes

boy is Bus - ter Brown, and the dog is Tige his friend, and they're

real-ly just a pic - ture, but it's fun to play pre - tend. So if

boys and girls like you, want some fun you'll get the shoe, with the

pic-ture of the boy, and the dog in-side, so you can put your foot in -

27

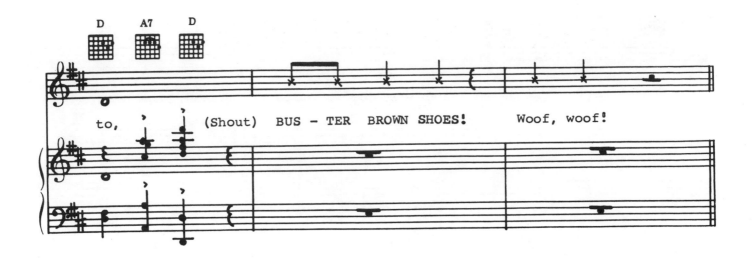

to, (Shout) BUS – TER BROWN SHOES! Woof, woof!

Buster Brown.®
AMERICA'S FAVORITE CHILDREN'S SHOES

This material is the exclusive property of the Brown Shoe Company Division of Brown Group, Inc., the owner of the federally-registered BUSTER BROWN trademark for children's shoes, which has consented to publication herein. Reproduction or other use without its permission is strictly prohibited.

Call For Philip Morris

Permission to reproduce granted by Philip Morris Incorporated

Catch A Cricket

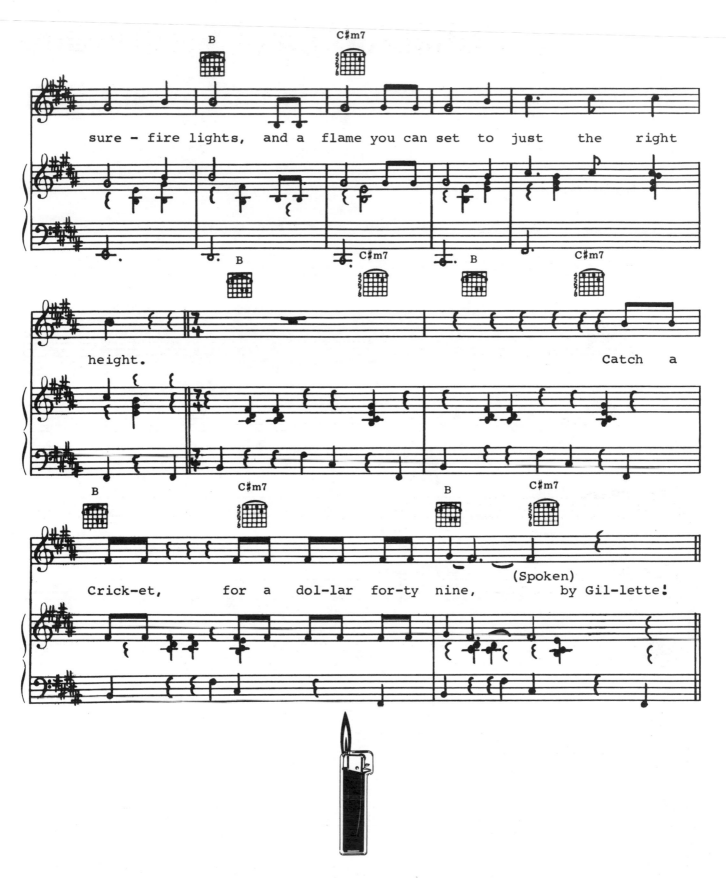

sure - fire lights, and a flame you can set to just the right height. Catch a Crick-et, for a dol-lar for-ty nine, (Spoken) by Gil-lette!

Reprinted with permission.
Copyright 1973 by The Gillette Company.
All rights reserved.

Chesterfield, Twenty-One Great Tobaccos

March tempo

(Shout)
Five, ten, fif-teen, twen-ty, Twen-ty- one great to-

bac- cos, make twen-ty won-der-ful smokes. Make your plea-sure true,

plea-sure long, plea-sure fil-ter free. Ches-ter- field, get the

Twen-ty one great to-bac-cos, make twen-ty won-der-ful smokes.

Twen-ty one great to-bac-cos, make twen-ty won-der-ful smokes. They're

blend-ed mild, not fil-tered mild, your plea-sure's fil-ter free.

Twen-ty one great to-bac-cos, make twen-ty won- der- ful smokes.

Permission to reproduce granted by Liggett Group Inc. All Rights Reserved.

Chock Full O' Nuts Is That Heavenly Coffee

Moderato

Chock Full O' Nuts is that hea-ven-ly cof-fee, hea-ven-ly

cof-fee, hea-ven-ly cof-fee, Chock Full O' Nuts is that hea-ven-ly

cof-fee, bet-ter cof-fee a mil-lion-aire's mon-ey can't buy.

Permission to reproduce granted by Chock Full O' Nuts

Come On Over
To The L&M Side

Permission to reproduce granted by Liggett Group Inc. All Rights Reserved.

36

Come Up To Kool

Permission to reproduce granted by Brown & Williamson Tobacco Corporation

Delta Is Ready When You Are

Del - ta is read - y to fly!

Copyright 1968 by Delta Air Lines, Inc.

Different Bites For Different Likes

Peter Paul

Written by Joey Levine

Rock beat

No-bod-y's quite the same,

There's diff-'rent bites for diff-'rent likes, I want York Mint Pat-tie and

he wants Pow-er-house, and she wants Car-a-velle, Oh, Oh well,

Permission to reproduce granted by Peter Paul, Inc.

Don't Think The Future

Lightly

Don't think the fu-ture is some-thing you can put off till to-mor-row, till to-mor-row, the fu-ture's Arm and Ham - mer.

Copyright 1976 by Church & Dwight Co., Inc.

Double Your Pleasure

Written by Mike Chan &
Dick Cunliffe

chew. So dou-ble your plea-sure, dou-ble your fun, Get dou-ble

ev-'ry-thing rolled in-to one, Oh, dou-ble your plea-sure,

Dou-ble your fun, with dou-ble good, dou-ble good, Dou-ble-mint Gum.

©Copyright 1959 by Wm. Wrigley, Jr. Company

Feelin' Free

Moderato with rock beat

There's a feel-in' a-round, it's A-mer-i-ca's sound, Pep-si

peo-ple feel-in' free,   Free to choose a new way,   free to

stand up and say, "You be you and I'll be me",   When you

46

All a-cross the na-tion, It's the Pep-si gen-er-a-tion here to-day, Here to stay, Feel-in' free.

Copyright 1973 by PepsiCo, Inc.

Fifty Million Times A Day

Brightly

Written by Ben Ludlow

"Coca-Cola" and "Coke" are the registered trademarks
which identify the same product of The Coca-Cola Company.

2) (Coca) Cola's as great as your first dancing date,
   As much fun as a day at the fair;
   For it gives you the gift of a bright little lift,
   That's as bracing as May morning air.   Fifty   (To Chorus)

3) (Coca) Cola's a thing that's eternally Spring,
   And its taste is as honest as truth;
   It's as sparkling and bright as a star spangled night,
   And as gay as the laughter of youth.   Fifty   (To Chorus)

Copyright 1955 by The Coca-Cola Company

Firestone Where The Rubber Meets The Road

Firestone

Permission to reproduce granted by The Firestone Tire & Rubber Company

First For Good Reason

HONDA

Words by Mike Navarro
Music by Dan Navarro

Moderato

1) Mo - vin' down the high-way, Won - d'rin' where the
2) Rid - in' in the o - pen, Know - in' who I

road will take me, Know I'm go - in' my way, 'cause I've got the
am, not hop - in', Rid - in' thru the ci - ty, Pass - in' cars, hey

wheels to make me free from wor - ry, free from care,
what a pi - ty they don't know a - bout my bike,

Permission to reproduce granted by American Honda Motor Company, Inc.

Ford, It's The Going Thing

Words by Murray Skurnick
Music by Stan Tarner

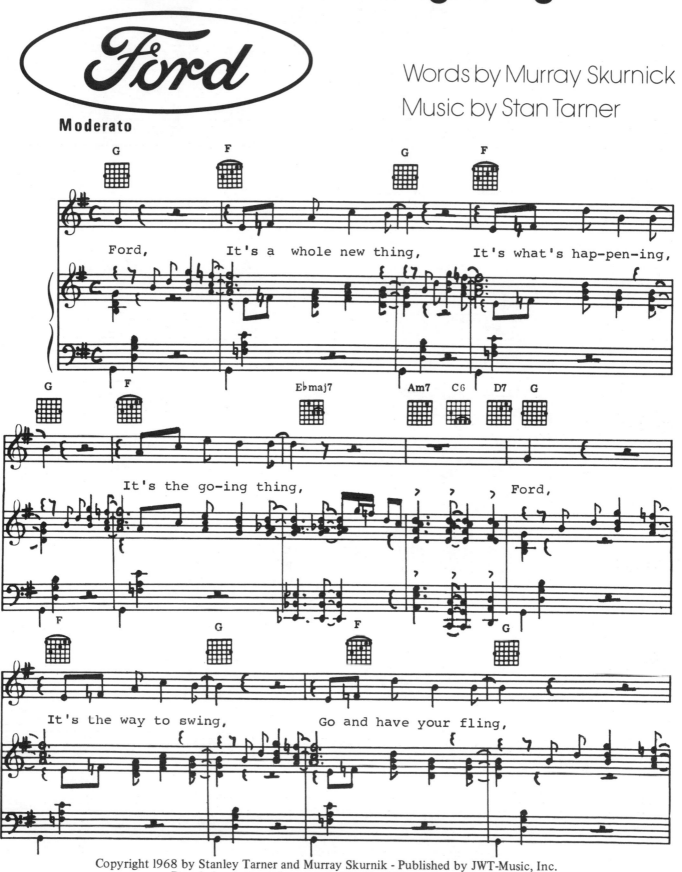

Copyright 1968 by Stanley Tarner and Murray Skurnik - Published by JWT-Music, Inc.
Permission to reproduce granted by Ford Motor Company

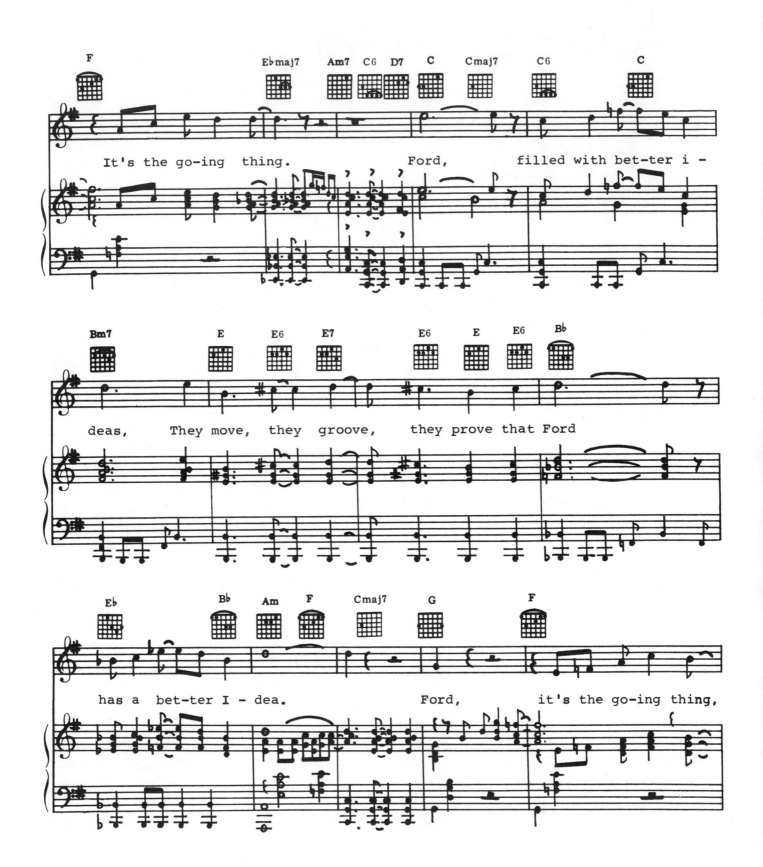

It's the go-ing thing. Ford, filled with bet-ter i-

deas, They move, they groove, they prove that Ford

has a bet-ter I - dea. Ford, it's the go-ing thing,

go, go, go-ing thing, It's the go-ing thing,

Yeah! Ford has a bet-ter i - dea, (It's the go - ing)

Gerber Knows
How Babies Grow

Lively

Ba-bies grow too fast for me, too fast, too fast, they grow to be, too big to bounce on Dad-dy's knee, Ba-bies grow too fast for me. For

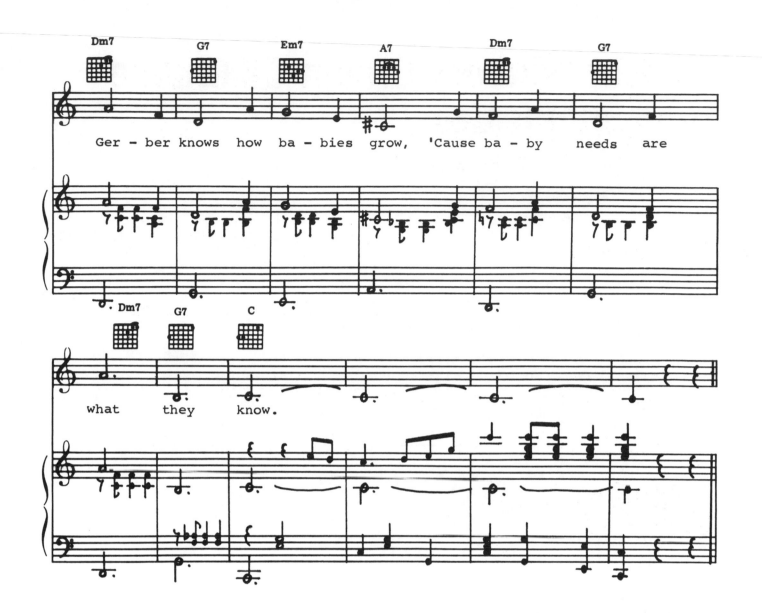

Ger - ber knows how ba - bies grow, 'Cause ba - by needs are
what they know.

Babies are our business...

Copyright 1965 & 1966 by Gerber Products Company

Get Wildroot Cream-Oil Charlie

Written by J. Ward Maurer

Get Wild - root Cream Oil, Char - lie, It keeps your hair in trim. You see it's non - al - co - hol - ic, Char - lie, it's made with sooth-ing lan - o - lin. You bet-ter get Wild - root

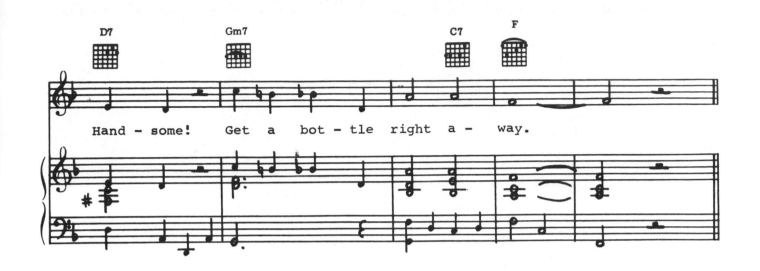

Hand - some! Get a bot - tle right a - way.

Copyright 1947 by Colgate-Palmolive Company

Gino's Gives You Freedom Of Choice

Gino's®

Written by Joey Levine

So, come on ev-'ry-bo-dy, and let's re-joice, yeah 'cause

Gi-no's gives you Free-dom of Choice.

Copyright 1975 by Gino's, Inc.

Greyhound's In Touch With America

Greyhound

Moderato

A - mer-i- ca, I've seen your joy in the fac-es of your peo -

ple, I've brought your sons and daugh-ters home from pla-ces far a-way,

Where-ev-er peo- ple want to go will be my des - tin- a -

68

Permission to reproduce granted by Grey-North, Inc.

Halo Everybody Halo

Brightly   Written by Joe Rines

Copyright 1946 & 1973 by Colgate-Palmolive Company

Have You Tried Wheaties

Barber shop quartet style

Have you tried Wheat-ies, They're whole wheat with all of the

bran. Won't you try Wheat-ies, for wheat is the best food of

man. They're cris-py, and crunch-y, the whole year through, the

72

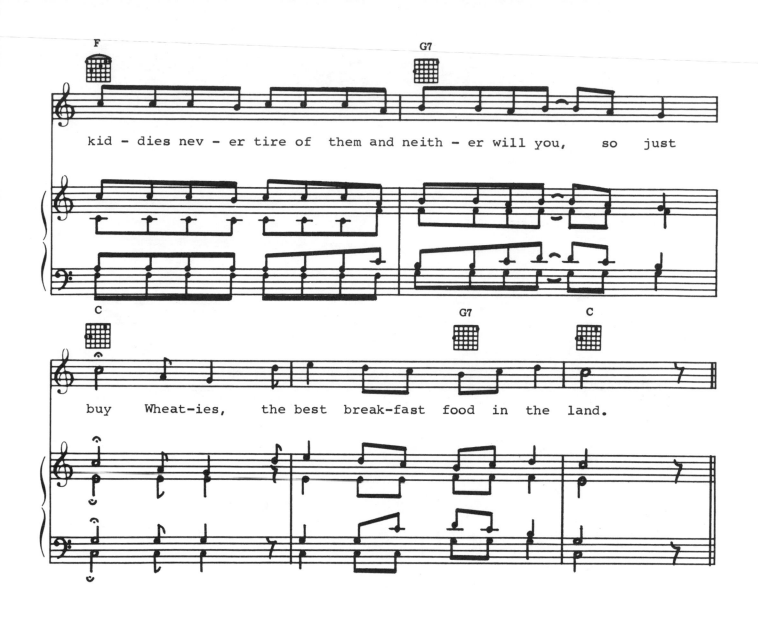

kid - dies nev - er tire of them and neith - er will you, so just

buy Wheat-ies, the best break-fast food in the land.

General Mills

Copyright 1929 by General Mills, Inc.

Hello Trees

HONDA
First. For good reason.

Written by Bob Menegger

Permission to reproduce granted by American Honda Motor Company, Inc.

Hey, Mabel, Black Label

"Carling Black Label" is a trademark owned and registered by Carling National Breweries, Inc.

Permission to reproduce granted by Carling National Breweries, Inc.

I Like Chiclets

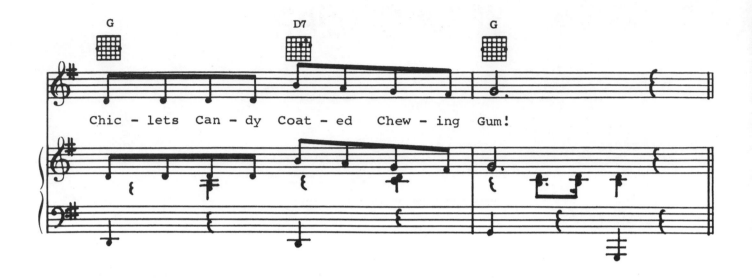

Chic - lets Can - dy Coat - ed Chew - ing Gum!

Chiclets ®

Permission to reproduce granted by Warner-Lambert Company

I Love Bosco

Bosco®
MILK AMPLIFIER
CHOCOLATE FLAVORED SYRUP

Written by Joan Edwards &
Lyn Duddy

Moderato

I love Bos - co, it's rich and choc - 'la - ty,

Choc - 'late flav - ored Bos - co, is might - y good for me.

Ma - ma puts it in my milk for ex - tra en - er - gy,

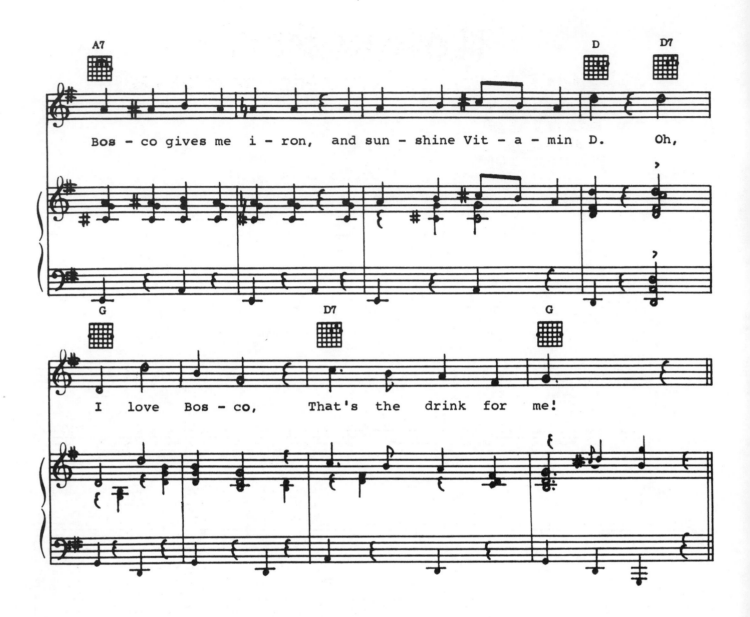

BOSCO®

MILK AMPLIFIER
CHOCOLATE FLAVORED SYRUP

Fortified with Vitamins
A, B₂, Niacin plus Iron

Copyright 1951 by Duet Music

The Wiener Song
(I Wish I Were An Oscar Mayer Wiener)

March tempo

Oh, I'd love to be an Os-car May-er wie-ner, That is what I'd
tru-ly like to be, 'Cause if I were an Os-car May-er wie - ner,
Ev-'ry-one would be in love with me. Oh, I'm glad I'm not an

Copyright 1965 by Oscar Mayer & Co. Inc., Madison, Wisconsin.
Reprinted with permission of the copyright owner.

If You've Got The Time, We've Got The Beer

Written by Bill Backer & McCann-Erickson, Inc.

Miller HIGH LIFE

The Champagne of Beers

85

Copyright 1971 by Miller Brewing Company

Chiquita Banana
(I'm Chiquita Banana)

Written by Len Mackenzie,
Garth Montgomery &
William Wirges

Calypso beat

I'm Chi-qui-ta Ba-na- na and I've come to say, I come from

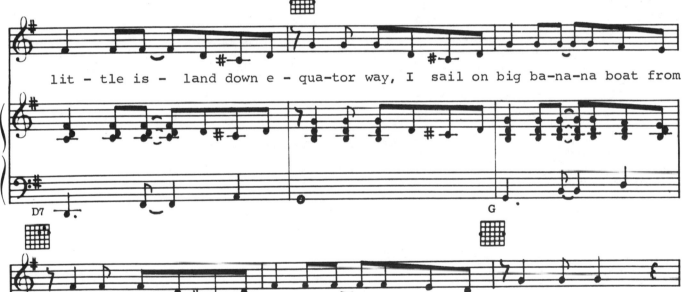

lit - tle is - land down e - qua-tor way, I sail on big ba-na-na boat from

Car-ri- bee, to see if I can help good neigh-bor pol - i- cee.

©Copyright 1946 by Shawnee Press, Inc., Delaware Water Gap, PA 18327. U.S. Copyright Renewed.
International Copyright Secured. All Rights Reserved. Used with permission.

na- nas,   And the re- frig - er - a - tor,   si, si, si, si.

*Registered trademark of United Brands Company.

Imprevu

Written by Geraci & Richards

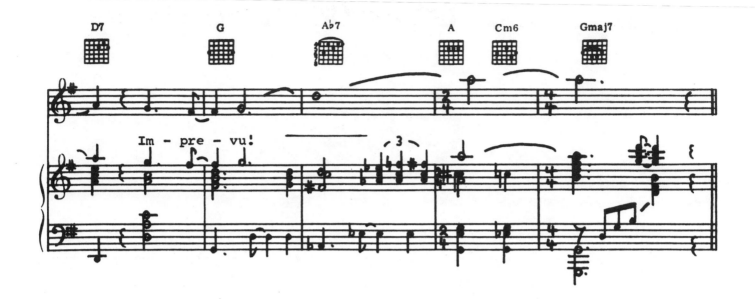

Imprévu

Copyright 1965 by Pfizer, Inc., New York, N.Y. 10017.
Reprinted with permission of Coty Division of Pfizer. All rights reserved.

It Tastes Too Good To Be True

Sugar Free

Written by Joe Brooks

Copyright 1974 by Light & Sound Co.
Permission to reproduce granted by Dr. Pepper Company. All rights reserved.

Copyright 1969 by The Coca-Cola Company

Kodak Makes Your Pictures Count

Written by Terry Cushman &
T. P. West

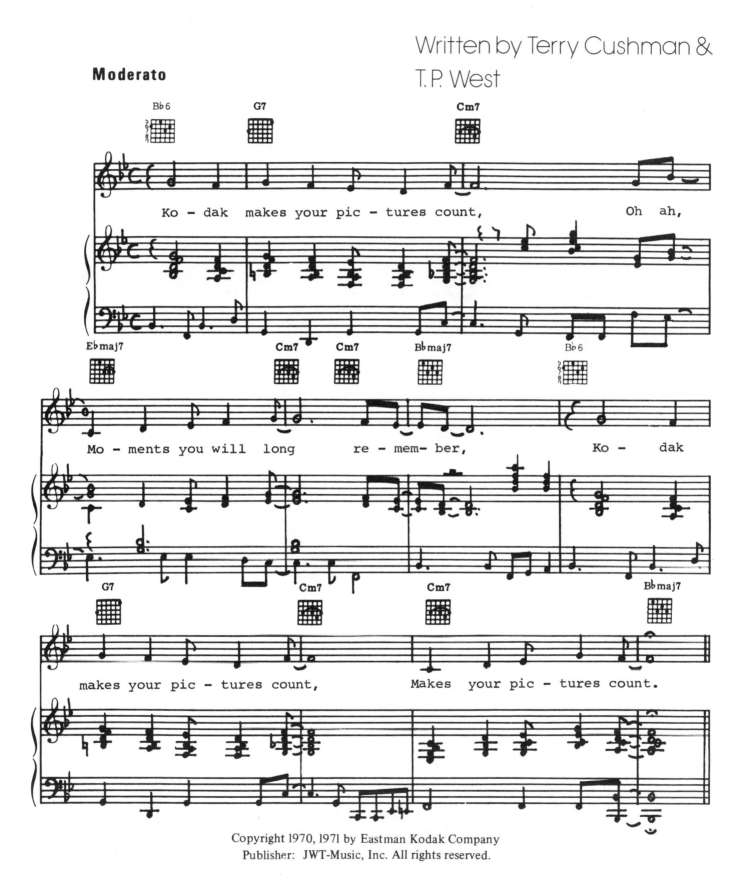

Copyright 1970, 1971 by Eastman Kodak Company
Publisher: JWT-Music, Inc. All rights reserved.

Let There Be Planters

Words by Jess Korman &
Nick Ullett
Music by Stan Tarner

Allegro

Let there be Plant-ers, let the good times in,

You don't need a par-ty for the fun to be-gin,

Let there be Plant - ers, let the good times in, when you

Let there be Plant-ers, Let there be Plant-ers, let the good times in.

Permission to reproduce granted by J. Walter Thompson Company

Let Your Fingers Do The Walking

yellow pages

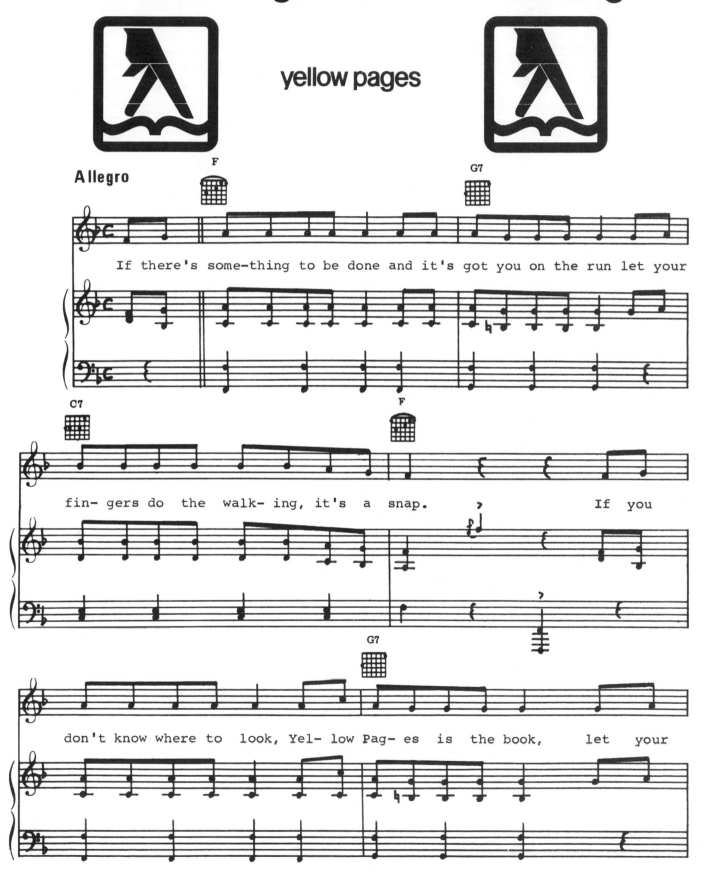

Permission to reproduce granted by American Telephone and Telegraph Company
and Cunningham & Walsh, Inc.

Life Savers

Slowly

Life Sav - ers, a part of liv - ing, 'cause their

great fla - vor has been a - round for years and years, And

folks have found there's noth - ing quite like Life Sav - ers,

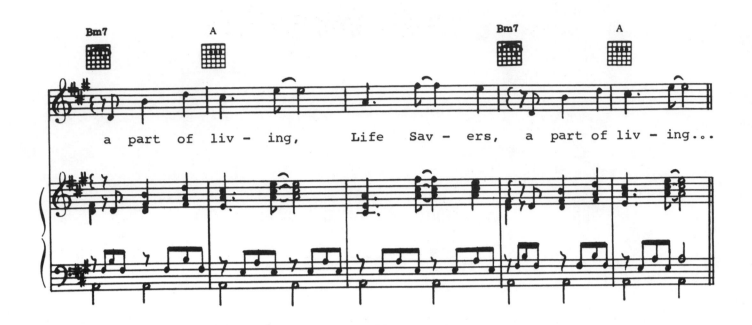

a part of liv - ing, Life Sav - ers, a part of liv - ing...

LIFE SAVERS ®

Copyright 1974 by Life Savers, Inc.
All rights reserved.

Like A Good Neighbor

Words by Jerry Gavin &
Keith Reinhard

Music by Barry Manilow

Moderato

We all hope the good times nev-er leave us be-hind,

We face our to-mor-rows, with some peace of mind,

But no man has a pro-mise of a life with-out care, and like a good

neigh-bor,   State Farm is there,   State Farm is there,   State Farm is

Copyright 1976 by G & W Publishing Corp.
c/o Publishers' Licensing Corporation, 488 Madison Ave., New York, N.Y. 10022.
All rights reserved. Used by permission.

Lipton Whistle Song

Allegretto

Written by Lee Schumer

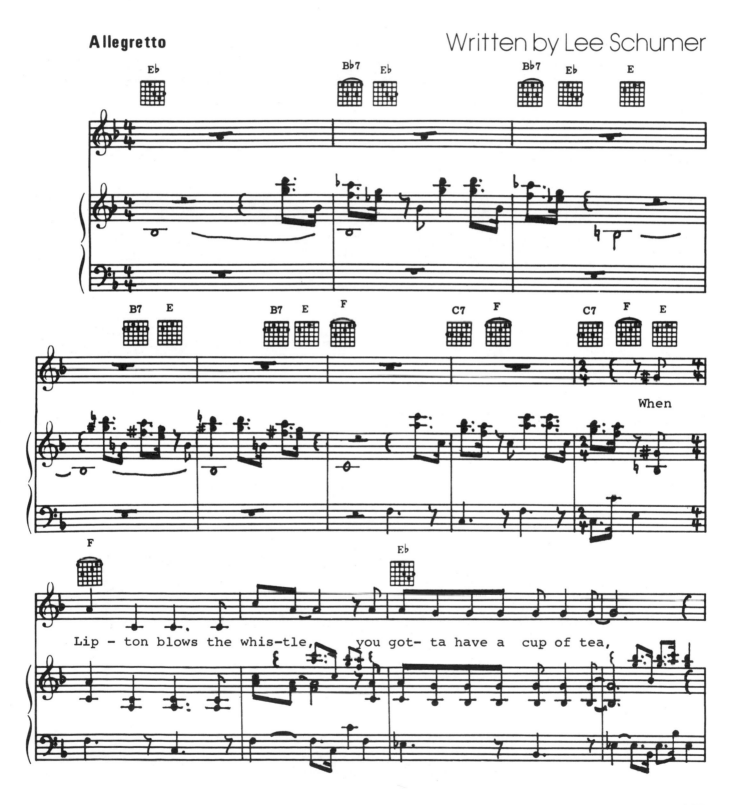

When

Lip - ton blows the whis-tle, you got- ta have a cup of tea,

Copyright 1972 by Thomas J. Lipton, Inc.

Love Your Hair

Written by James Neal Harvey

Copyright 1974 by James Neal Harvey, Inc.

Man Oh Manischewitz

Written by Myron Mahler

Moderato

Man-i-schew-itz is the wine for you, Man-i-schew-itz lets the fla-vor through. Goes down smooth, tastes good too, the best there is, Man-i-schew-itz'-s, Man-o- Man-i-schew-itz what a wine!

Permission to reproduce granted by Savitt Tobias Balk, Inc.

Me And My R C

Moderato

My face is freck-led from the sun, got a strong wind in my hair, the

bike feels warm and we're far from home, and we sure don't have a care. I

take my R. C. Co - la most ev - 'ry - where we ride,

Permission to reproduce granted by Royal Crown Cola Co.

Milk Is A Natural

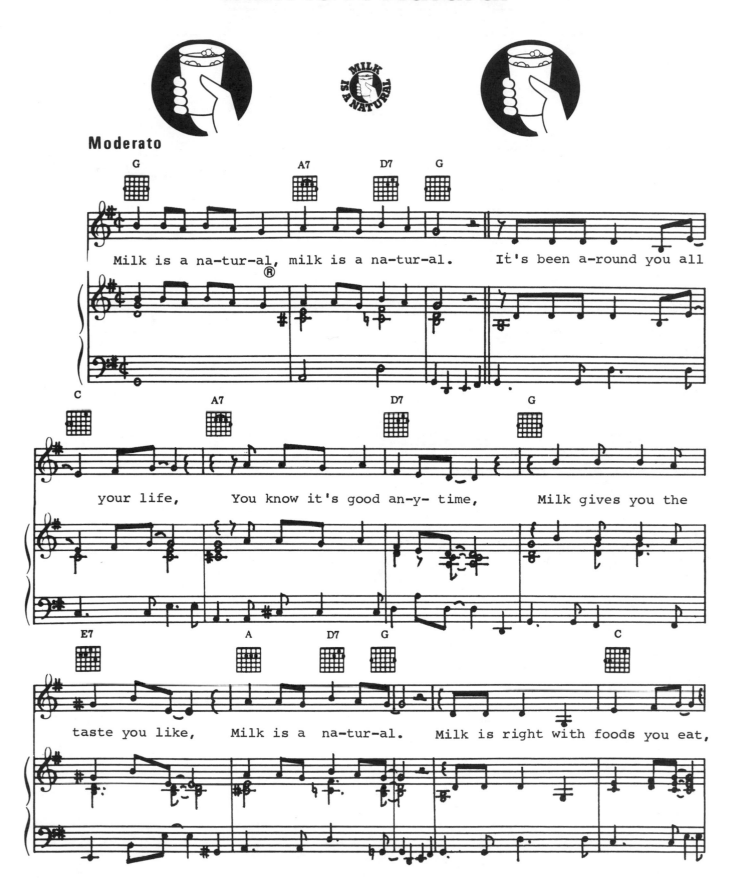

Moderato

Milk is a na-tur-al, milk is a na-tur-al. It's been a-round you all your life, You know it's good an-y- time, Milk gives you the taste you like, Milk is a na-tur-al. Milk is right with foods you eat,

114

american dairy association®

Permission to reproduce granted by American Dairy Association

115

MMM, MMM, Good

Campbell Soup Company

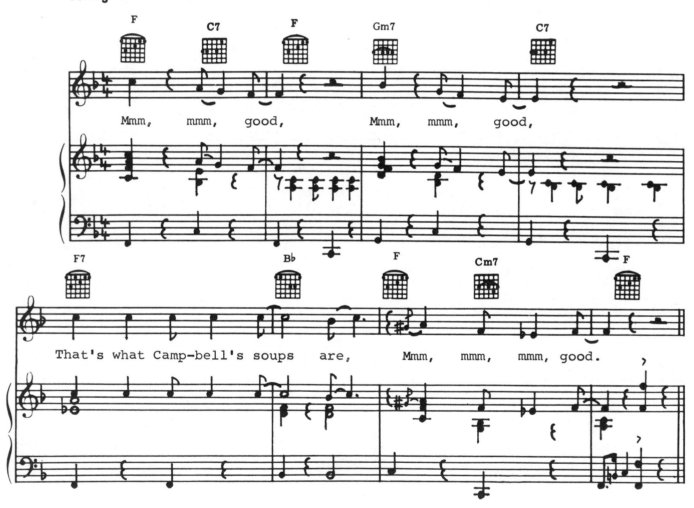

Permission to reproduce granted by Campbell Soup Company

Most Misunderstood Soft Drink

Written by Joe Brooks

117

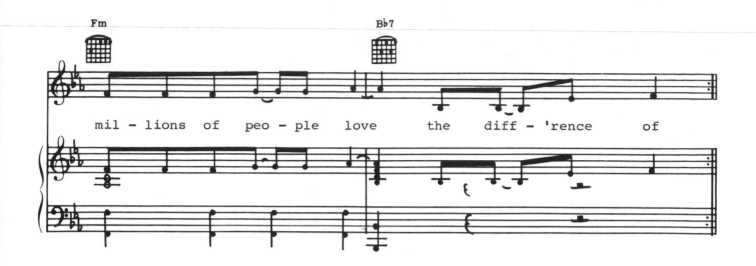

mil – lions of peo – ple love the diff – 'rence of

Copyright 1971-1973 by Light & Sound Co.
Permission to reproduce granted by Dr. Pepper Company. All rights reserved.

Most Original Soft Drink Ever

Written by Randy Newman

Additional lyrics by Jake Holmes

This old world keeps turn-ing, and most folks fol - low a-long, But some got-ta play their own way, Got-ta sing a dif-f'rent song, They give life its fla-vor, a lit-tle

Copyright 1974 by Randy Newman
Permission to reproduce granted by Dr. Pepper Company. All rights reserved.

Mother Country

UNITED AIRLINES

Written by United Airlines

Have you seen the oth-er side of where you live,

Don't you know this great big land has got so much to give,

Mo - ther Coun-try's got her arms o - pen wide, Don't let your

Copyright 1973 by United Airlines. All rights reserved.

Mutual Of Omaha
People You Can Count On

Words by Jerry Gavin
Music by Sid Woloshin

Slowly

You got-ta make it, you got-ta make your way and care e-nough,

So things keep go- ing, when the times get rough,

You got-ta take it, the trou-ble you can bet - 'll

Permission to reproduce granted by Mutual of Omaha Insurance Company

My Beer Is Rheingold The Dry Beer

German waltz style

My beer is Rhein-gold, the dry beer, Think of Rhein-gold, when-

ev- er you buy beer, It's re- fresh-ing, not sweet, it's the

ex-tra dry treat, won't you try Ex-tra Dry Rhein-gold Beer.

Permission to reproduce granted by Chock Full O' Nuts

127

Never Borrow Money Needlessly

Written by Bill Walker

Permission to reproduce granted by Household Finance Corporation

Next Best Thing To Your Good Cooking

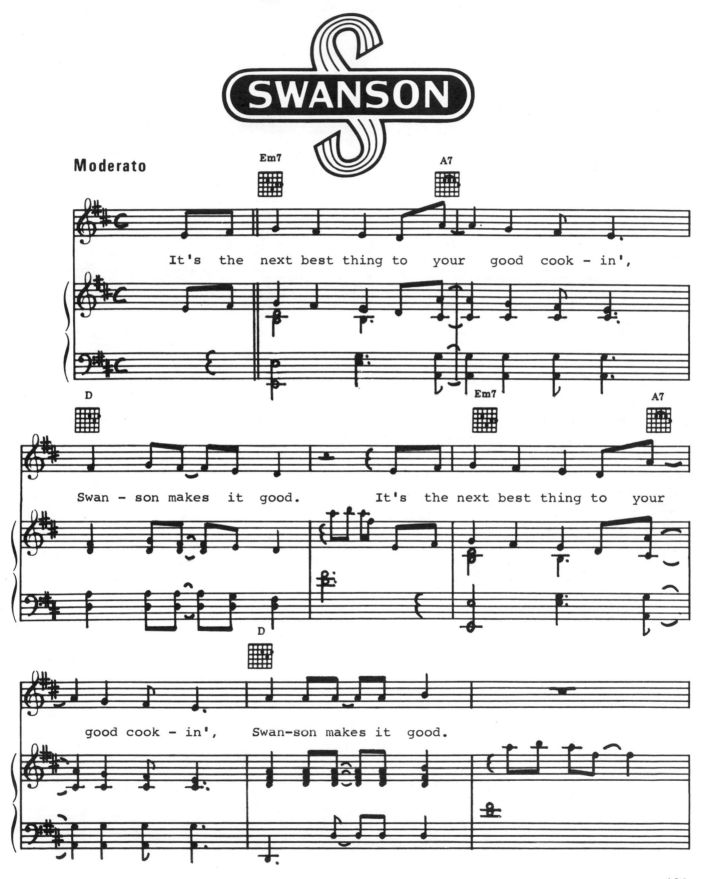

Copyright 1971 by The Campbell Soup Company

130

Nobody Doesn't Like Sara Lee

KITCHENS OF
Sara Lee

Ⓒ A CONSOLIDATED FOODS COMPANY • RESPONSIVE TO CONSUMER NEEDS

Moderato

Permission to reproduce granted by Kitchens of Sara Lee. All Rights Reserved. Used with permission.

Nothing Goes With Everything
Like Mueller's

Written by Phyllis Levinson &
Neil Warner

Allegretto

More peo-ple eat Muel-ler's than an-y oth-er brand,

All a-cross this beau-ti-ful land, and they've been eat-ing Muel-ler's a

hun-dred years or so, May-be that's be-cause ev-'ry-bo-dy knows that

Copyright 1975 by C. F. Mueller Company.
Permission to reproduce granted by C. F. Mueller Company.

Muel-ler's Egg Nood-les real-ly make a meal com-plete.

Noth-ing goes with ev-'ry-thing like Muel-ler's, It goes with ev-'ry-thing.

Old Spice

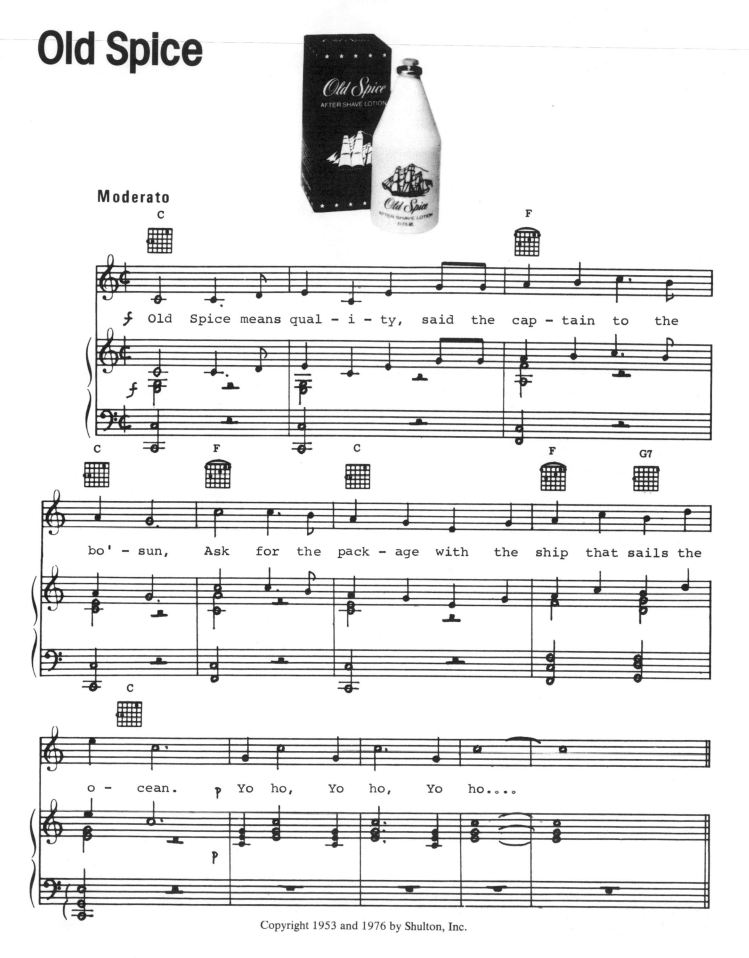

Moderato

Old Spice means qual-i-ty, said the cap-tain to the bo'-sun, Ask for the pack-age with the ship that sails the o-cean. Yo ho, Yo ho, Yo ho....

Copyright 1953 and 1976 by Shulton, Inc.

Only Mustang Makes It Happen

Words by Murray Skurnick &
Jerry Sussman
Music by Stan Tarner

Copyright 1976 by Ford Motor Company - published by JWT-Music, Inc.
Permission to reproduce granted by Ford Motor Company

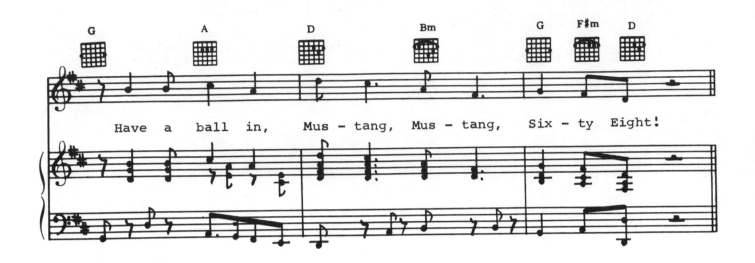

Have a ball in, Mus - tang, Mus - tang, Six - ty Eight!

FORD DIVISION

Our L'eggs Fit Your Legs

Written by Tom Dawes

Moderato

L'eggs are here, L'eggs are there, L'eggs are ev-'ry-where,

Our L'eggs fit your legs, they hug you, they hold you, they

nev-er let you go. Get 'em at the L'eggs Bou-tique!

Permission to reproduce granted by L'eggs Products, Inc.

139

Pabst Blue Ribbon Beer

Moderato

Out of the past comes Pabst Blue Rib-bon, Smooth-er, rich-er,

fin - er fla-vor, What-'ll ya have, old time fla-vor,

Pabst Blue Rib-bon Beer, O-rig-i-nal Pabst! Blue Rib-bon

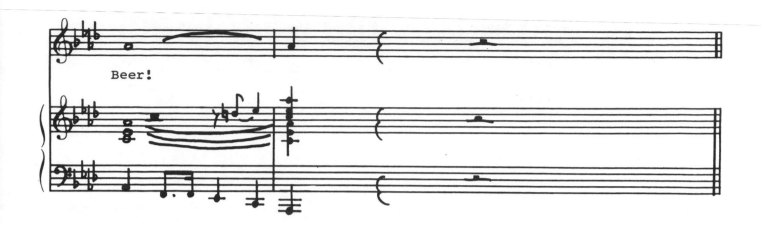

Beer!

Permission to reproduce granted by Pabst Brewing Company

Pan Am Makes The Goin' Great

Words by Warren Pfaff
Music by Stan Applebaum

Allegro

Makes the go - in' great!

Copyright 1967 by Tod Music, Inc.

Pennzoil Please

Words by Ronald Lee Phillips
Music by John Andrew Tartaglia

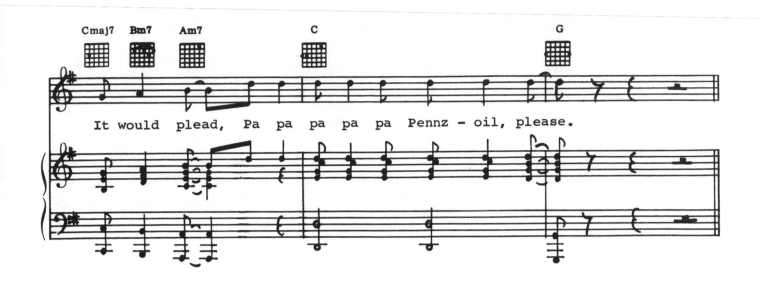

It would plead, Pa pa pa pa pa Pennz - oil, please.

Permission to reproduce granted by Pennzoil Company

Pepsi-Cola Hits The Spot

Brightly

Copyright 1940 by Pepsi-Cola Company

Pepsi's Got A Lot To Give
You've Got A Lot To Live

Words by Batten, Barton Durstine & Osborn

Music by Joe Brooks

There's a whole new way of liv-in', Pep-si helps sup-ply the drive, it's got a lot to give to those who like to live 'cause Pep-si helps 'em come a-live, It's the

Copyright 1969 by PepsiCo, Inc.

Pillsbury Says It Best

Written by
Leo Burnett Company, Inc.

A house ain't a home 'til you bake in the o-ven, a cake in the o-ven, a pie in the o-ven, Noth-in' says lov-in' like some-thin' from the o-ven, and Pills-bu-ry says it best. A

home smells so nice when you bake in the o - ven, Cook-ies in the o-ven,

Rolls in the o-ven, Noth-in' says lov-in' like some-thin' from the o-ven, and

Pills-bu-ry says it best! Wheth-er you bake a lit-tle or a lot,

Whe-ther you make it fan-cy or not, you please your fam-i-ly, you

Copyright 1957, 1958 by The Pillsbury Company, formerly Pillsbury Mills, Inc.
Reproduced with permission of The Pillsbury Company, which reserves all rights.

Plymouth Is Out To Win You Over

Plymouth

Written by Artie Fields

CHRYSLER CORPORATION

Jazz waltz style

Ply-mouth is out to win you ov – er this year.

Ply-mouth is out to win you ov – er this year.

Fol – low your heart, see your Ply – mouth deal – er to –

CHRYSLER CORPORATION

Permission to reproduce granted by Chrysler Corporation

Pow, Pow, Powerful

Rock beat

Gon - na get a pow - er - ful start to - day,

Gon - na have some pow - er - ful good Cheer - i - os, Gon - na get a

pow, pow, pow - er - ful good, good, feel - ing from Cheer, Cheer, Cheer - i - os,

Permission to reproduce granted by General Mills, Inc.

Propa P.H.

BIO PRODUCTS INC

Rock beat

Grow-in' up can real-ly up-set your face, Your

mir-ror can be-come an aw-ful, mean and ug-ly place,

So don't let an up-set face, Real-ly get you down,

Help clear it up with Pro - pa P. H.

Permission to reproduce granted by Bio Products, Inc.

Put A Tic Tac In Your Mouth

Written by Bob Hildt,
Frank Nicholo, Neil Warner &
Larry Levinson

Moderato

Put a Tic Tac in your mouth and get a bang out of life, It's a clean fresh ex- plo-sion of mint, Put a Tic Tac in your mouth and get a bang out of life, it's a clean fresh ex- plo- sion of mint. Put a

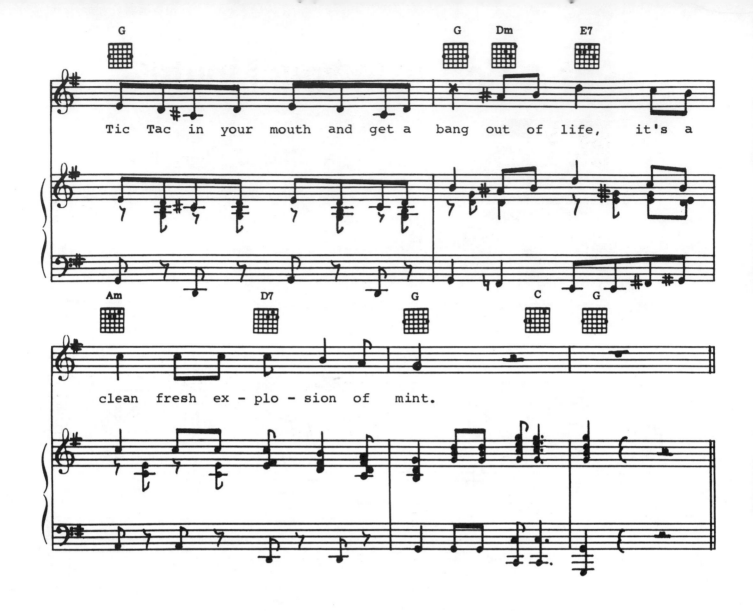

Permission to reproduce granted by Ferrero U.S.A.

Real Goodness™ From Kentucky Fried Chicken®

Words by Hal Kome
Music by Comtrack, Inc.

Rock beat

Look at this, this is cook-in', it's a meal, Oh, Real Good-ness from the Colo-nel, here's a meal, "It's fin-ger lick-in' good," so you know it's all right,

Copyright 1975 by KFC National Cooperative Advertising Program, Inc.

Real Goodness
Kentucky Fried Chicken ®

Rinso White

Registered trademark of Lever Brothers Company

Roto-Rooter

Moderato

When Ro - to Root - er comes, That's when your trou - bles go,

When Ro - to Root - er's here, That's when your trou - bles dis -

ap - pear. Call Ro - to Root - er, that's the name, and a -

way go trou - bles down the drain. Ro - to Root - er, sew-er ser-vice,

Ro - to Root - er, Ro - to Root - er, Ro - to Root - er....

Permission to reproduce granted by Roto-Rooter Corporation

Schaefer Is The One Beer

Words by Jim Jordan
Music by Joe Hornsby &
Ted German

Copyright 1967 by The F. & M. Schaefer Brewing Co.

Sears Where America Shops

Words by Noel Digby &
Gus Chan

Music by Dick Marx

And Sears is to-day. Sears is where A- mer-i- ca shops,

For the life we lead, Sears is where A - mer- i - ca shops,

For the things we need. Sears is the name that means real

val- ue, Sears is the name that you can trust.

Permission to reproduce granted by Sears, Roebuck and Co.

See The U.S.A. In Your Chevrolet

Chevrolet

Written by Leon Carr &
Leo Corday

March tempo

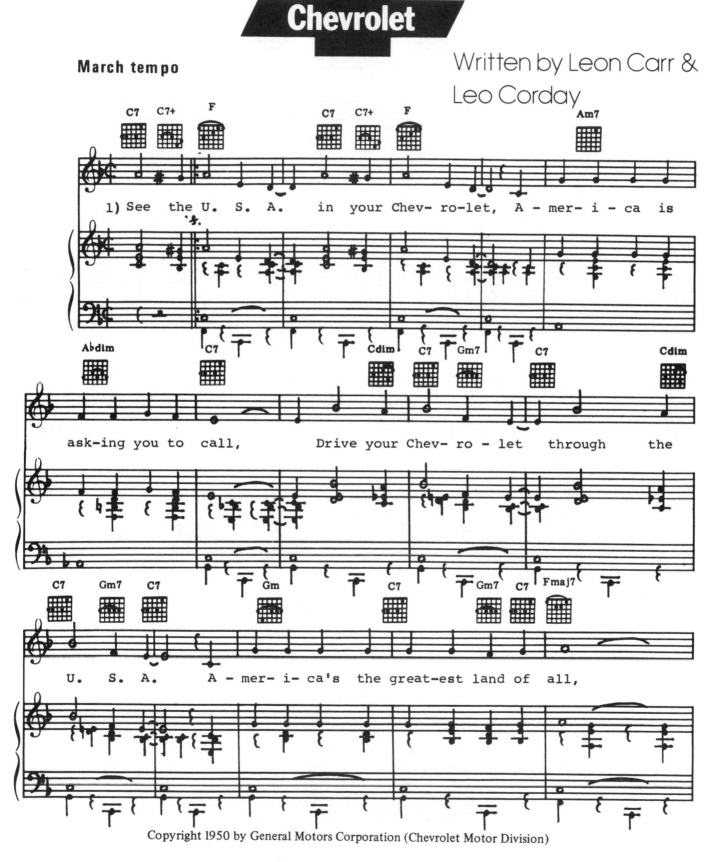

1) See the U. S. A. in your Chev-ro-let, A-mer-i-ca is ask-ing you to call, Drive your Chev-ro-let through the U. S. A. A-mer-i-ca's the great-est land of all,

Copyright 1950 by General Motors Corporation (Chevrolet Motor Division)

(D.S. - 2nd Verse)

Second Verse

See the U.S.A. in your Chevrolet,
The Rockies way out West are calling you,
Drive your Chevrolet through the U.S.A.,
Where waving fields of wheat pass in review.
Whether trav'ling light or with a load that's heavy,
Performance is sweeter, nothing can beat 'er,
Life is completer in a Chevy.
So make a date today, to see the U.S.A.,
And see it in your Chevrolet.

Seven Kinds Of Fruit In Hawaiian Punch

Copyright 1975 by Sunday Productions, Inc. & RJR Foods, Inc.

Snap, Crackle & Pop

Written by N. B. Winkless, Jr.

® Kellogg Company

Copyright 1961 by Kellogg Company

177

Soft, Strong, Pops Up Too

Allegretto

Soft, strong, pops up too, Kleen - ex® tis-sues are made for you. When you're caught with a sud - den sneeze, Kleen-ex serves you with speed and ease. Soft, strong, pops up too,

Permission to reproduce granted by Kimberly-Clark Corporation

Sometimes I Feel Like A Nut

Permission to reproduce granted by Peter Paul, Inc.

Sound Off For Chesterfield

Written by Willie Lee Duckworth &
Bernard Lentz

Lyrics:

It's Ches-ter-field you ought to buy, we kid you not, they sat-is-fy, They're mild and tast-y, ev-'ry puff, for pure smok-ing plea-sure, sure e-nough. Ask the man in an-y shop, for

Copyright 1950 by Bernard Lentz.
Assigned to and Copyright 1951, 1960 and 1961 by Shapiro, Bernstein & Co., Inc.,
New York, New York 10022. All rights reserved. Used by permission.
Permission to reproduce granted by Liggett Group Inc. All Rights Reserved.

Stay Close To Someone

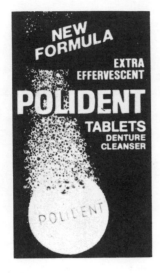

Written by Michael Cohen

Slowly

Stay close to some-one to laugh with and cry on, Stay close to some-one to love and re-ly on, Stay close to some - one.

Copyright 1975 by Grey Advertising Inc.

Take Life A Little Easier

Words by John Annarino
Music by Sid Woloshin

Copyright 1972 by G & W Publishing Corp. c/o
Publishers' Licensing Corporation, 488 Madison Avenue, New York, N.Y. 10022.
All rights reserved. Used by permission.

Tan Don't Burn
Get A
Coppertone Tan

Make the most of mo - ments in the sun,

Cop - per - tone makes liv - in' in the sun - shine fun, it

gives the fast - est tan as you will quick - ly see, 'cause

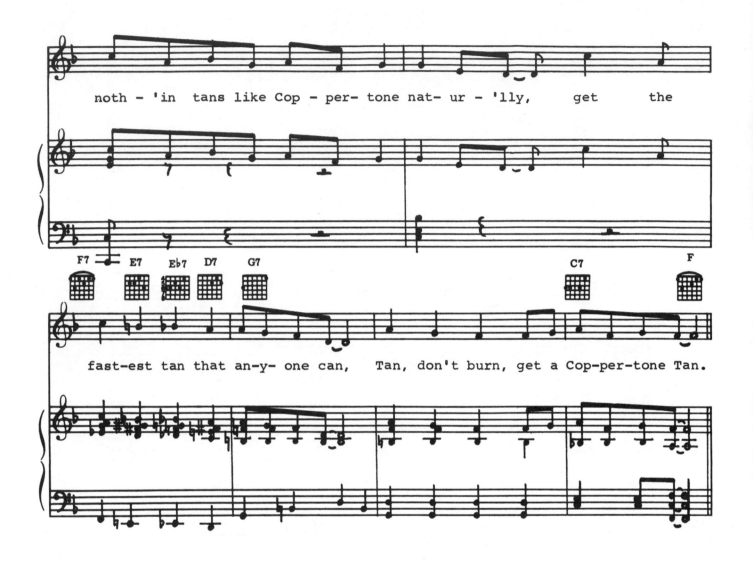

noth – 'in tans like Cop – per– tone nat– ur – 'lly, get the

fast–est tan that an–y– one can, Tan, don't burn, get a Cop–per–tone Tan.

Coppertone®

Permission to reproduce granted by Plough, Inc.

The Big Red Team

March tempo

Copyright 1975 by The Great Atlantic and Pacific Tea Company

The Dogs Kids Love To Bite
(Armour Hot Dog Theme)

Written by Clay Warnick

Moderato

Hot dogs, Ar - mour hot dogs, what do kids put on Ar - mour

hot dogs? Mus - tard, ket - chup, lots of rel - ish too,

pick - les, on - ions, e - ven pea-nut but-ter too on hot dogs, Ar-mour

Copyright 1968 by Armour and Company

ARMOUR

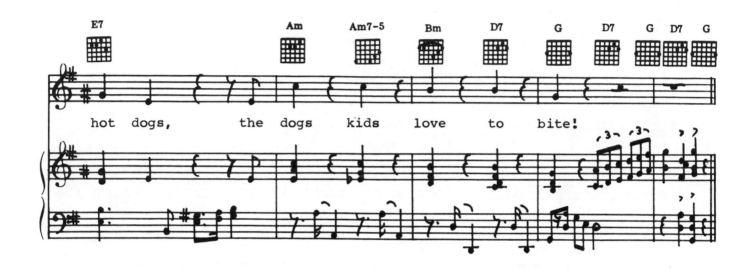

hot dogs,   the dogs   kids   love   to   bite!

Texaco Star Theme
(The Man Who Wears The Star)

Written by W. A. Fredricks

We are the Men of Tex-a-co, We wear the Tex-a-co Star. We like to think at Tex-a-co, We've got ev-'ry-thing for your car! We've got wi-pers for your

wind-shield, plugs 'n' belts 'n' ti – res too, Lub – ri – cants and

bat – ter – ies and pol-ish-es for you, All the things to keep your en-gine

up to par, we've got ev -'ry - thing for your car. That's why

you can trust your car, to the man who wears the star, for the kind of

prod-ucts that can take care of your car, at ev-'ry Tex - a - co sta-tion, clean a - cross the na - tion, You can trust your car to the man who wears the star, the big, bright Tex-a- co Star!

Copyright 1961 by Texaco Inc.

The Thracian Horse Music
(Budweiser Theme Song)

Budweiser
KING OF BEERS®

Permission to reproduce granted by Anheuser-Busch, Inc.

There Is Nothing Like A Lark

Moderato

There is noth-ing like a Lark, noth-ing like a Lark, noth-ing like a

Lark.   All a- round this big coun- try,   from Maine to Mon-ter- ey,

Lark tastes so much smooth-er, You're like-ly to hear a lot of folks

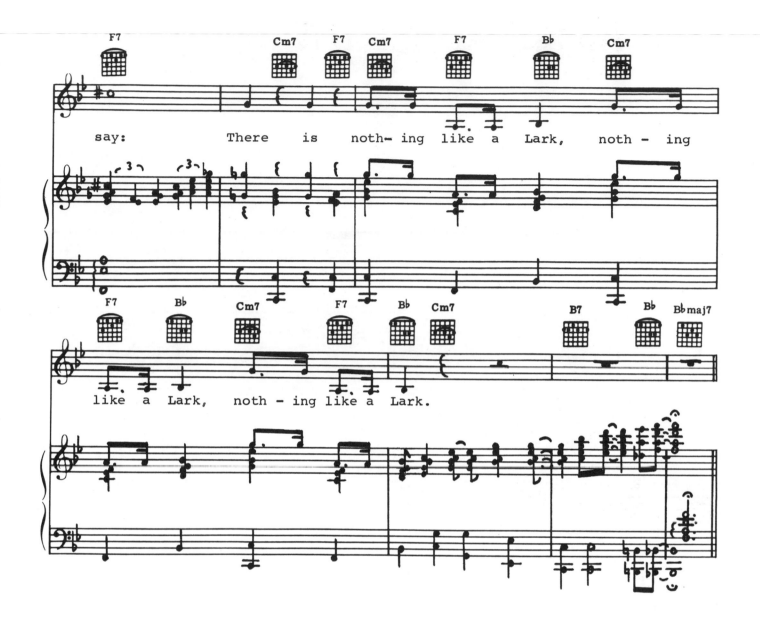

LARK

Permission to reproduce granted by Liggett Group Inc. All Rights Reserved.

Things Go Better With Coke

Trademark ®

Written by Bill Backer

Moderato

Things go bet-ter with Co-ca Co-la, Things go bet-ter with Coke, Life is much more fun when you're re-freshed, And Coke re-fresh-es you best. It's the re-fresh-ing-est!

"Coca-Cola" and "Coke" are the registered trademarks
which identify the same product of The Coca-Cola Company.

Copyright 1963 by The Coca-Cola Company

This Is The L&M Moment

Words by Jess Korman
Music by Stan Tarner

Lyrics:
This is the L & M Mo - ment, This is the L & M Mo - ment,

D.C. al Fine
Repeat and fade

Permission to reproduce granted by Liggett Group Inc. All Rights Reserved.

To Look Sharp

Registered Trademark of The Gillette Company

Written by Mahlon Merrick

March tempo

Look sharp, feel sharp, be sharp! To

look sharp, ev-'ry time you shave, to feel sharp,

And be on the ball, Just be sharp, use Gil-

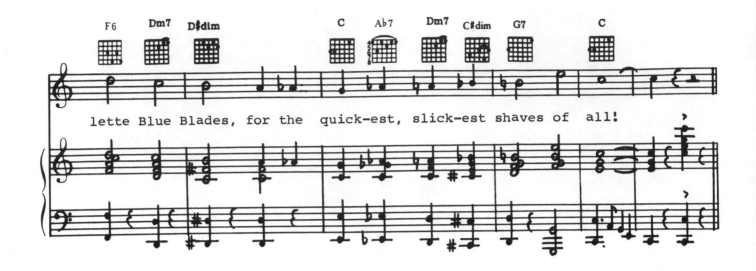

lette Blue Blades, for the quick-est, slick-est shaves of all!

SHARPIE

Reprinted with permission.
Copyright 1953 by The Gillette Company and Mahlon Merrick.
All rights reserved.

Tootsie Roll Lasts A Long Time

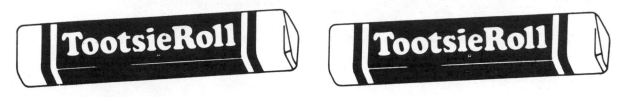

Permission to reproduce granted by Tootsie Roll Industries, Inc.

Two Great Tastes

Allegretto

You get Two great tastes in one can-dy bar, Rees-es
Pea-nut But-ter Cup. La, la, la, la, la, la, la, la, la, la,
la, la la, You get two great tastes in one

Copyright 1970 by Hershey Foods Corporation

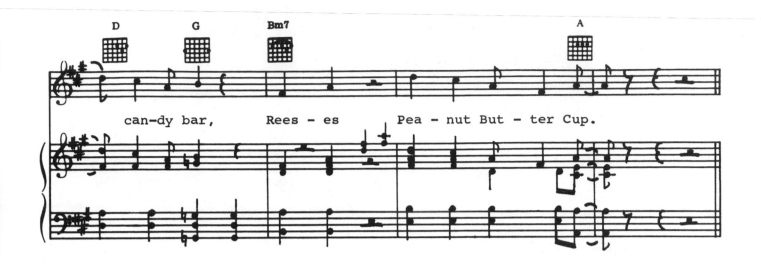

can-dy bar, Rees - es Pea - nut But - ter Cup.

Union Label

Words by Paula Green
Music by Malcolm Dodds

March tempo

Look for the un-ion la - bel, when you are buy - ing a

coat, dress, or blouse. Re - mem-ber some-where, our un-ion's

sew - ing, our wag-es go -ing, to feed the kids and run the house, we

work hard, but who's com-plain-ing, Thanks to the I. L. G. we're

pay-ing our way, So, al-ways look for the un-ion la-bel,

It says we're a-ble to make it in the U. S. A.

Copyright 1975 by International Ladies' Garment Workers' Union
Permission to reproduce granted by Green Dolmatch Inc.

Use Ajax The Foaming Cleanser

AJAX

Written by Joe Rines

Allegro

(Boom, boom, boom, boom, boom, boom, boom,) Use A- jax (Boom,

boom), the foam-ing clean-ser, (Boom, boom, boom, boom, boom, boom, boom)

Floats the dirt right down the drain! (Boom, boom, boom, boom, boom, boom)

boom, boom, boom, boom, boom, boom, boom) You'll stop pay- ing the

el - bow tax, when you start clean - ing with A - jax. So use

A-jax (boom boom) the foam-ing clean-ser (boom boom boom boom boom boom boom)

Floats the dirt right down the drain! (Boom, boom, boom, boom, boom, boom, boom!)

Copyright 1950 by Colgate-Palmolive Company

VICEROY

Viceroy Gives You All The Taste All The Time

Words by Richard Delia
Music by Stan Applebaum

Don't set-tle for some of the taste, some of the time,

Vice-roy gives you all the taste, all the time.

Copyright 1969 by Tod Music, Inc.

Westinghouse Makes It Happen

Written by Morty Jay

Moderato

West-ing-house helps make it hap-pen! West-ing-house

helps make it hap-pen! Start-ing the nu-cle-ar age.

Pow-er that can make things go, That the na-tion needs to grow.

Pow- er that can build a bet- ter, rich- er age.

West- ing- house helps make it hap - pen! Stretch- ing our

fuel en- er- gy. This will be a bet- ter land, bright- er

and a clean- er land, with the switch to e- lec- tric e- con- o-

my. When build-ers make new ci- ties grow, they need to

keep the cost down low, Who helps make it hap - pen,

West- ing-house, new ways to move a- round the town, from home to work,

and up and down. Who helps make it hap-pen? West-ing-house.

217

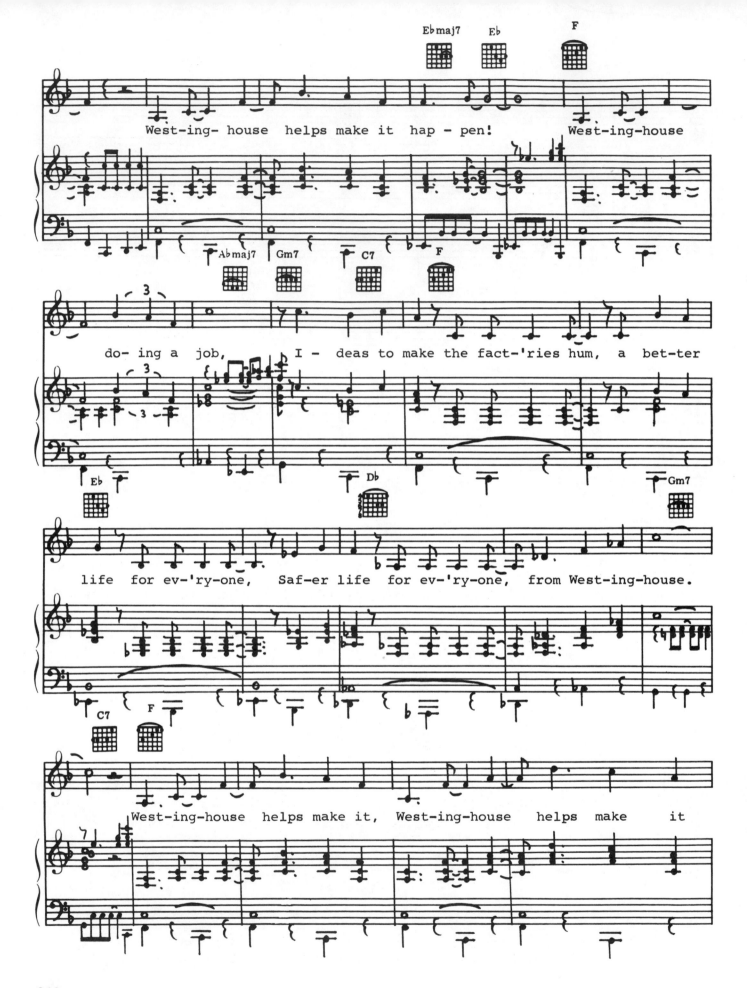

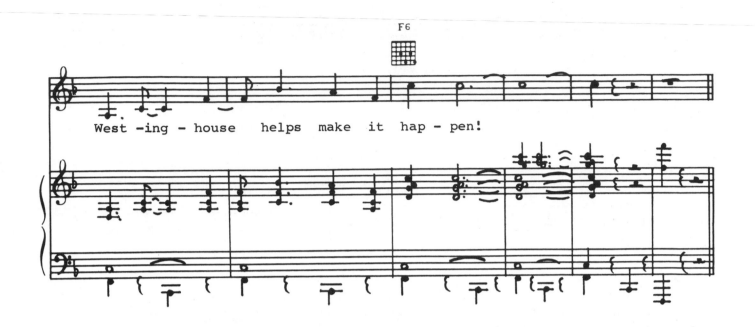

West -ing - house   helps   make   it   hap - pen!

Permission to reproduce granted by Westinghouse Electric Corporation

When The Values Go Up!

When the val-ues go up, up, up! And the pri-ces go down, down, down! Rob-ert Hall this sea-son will show you the rea - son,

©ROBERT HALL CLOTHES, INC.
Copyright 1946, 1954, 1963 and 1972 by Robert Hall Clothes, Inc.

Low o - ver-head,   Low o - ver - head!

® *Robert Hall*

A DIVISION OF UNITED MERCHANTS

Where There's Life, There's Bud

Budweiser
KING OF BEERS®

Words by Bob Johnson
Music by Russ David

Where there's life there's Bud, In a pent-house or a bun-ga-low, where the bright sun shines or can-dles glow, Bud-wei-ser Beer is for folks who know, Where there's life there's Bud.

Copyright 1959 by D'Arcy Advertising Company

Winston Tastes Good
Winston

Moderato

Win-ston tastes good like a cig-ar-ette should, Win-ston tastes

good, like a (clap-clap) cig-ar-ette should. Win-ston gives you

real fla-vor, full, rich to-bac-co fla-vor, Win-ston's eas-y

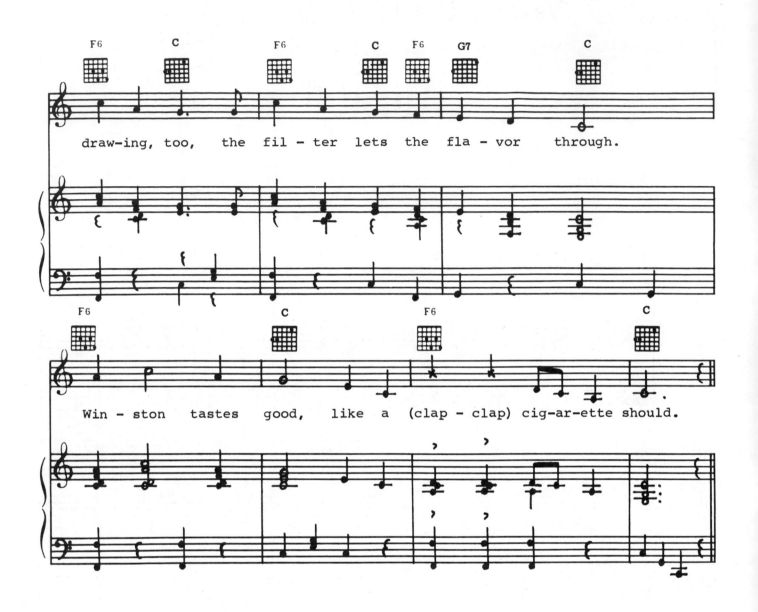

draw-ing, too, the fil – ter lets the fla – vor through.

Win – ston tastes good, like a (clap – clap) cig-ar-ette should.

Copyright 1976 by R.J. Reynolds Tobacco Co.
Permission to reproduce granted by R.J. Reynolds Tobacco Co. All rights reserved.

Wouldn't You Really Rather Have A Buick

Moderato

Would-n't you real-ly rath-er have a Bu-ick, a

Bu-ick, a Bu-ick? Would-n't you real-ly rath-er have a

Bu-ick this year!

Permission to reproduce granted by McCann-Erickson, Inc.

You Deserve A Break Today®

Words by Keith Reinhard,
Richard Hazlett & Ed Farran
Music by Sid Woloshin &
Kevin Gavin

Allegro

So much life to be lived, So much to be tried,

And when you share it you get, A spec-ial feel-ing in-side,

It's a full-time thing, The kind of life that you lead,

Copyright 1971 by G & W Publishing Corp. c/o Publishers' Licensing Corporation, 488 Madison Ave., NY, NY 10022. All rights reserved. Used by permission.
Permission to reproduce granted by McDonald's Corporation.
®- Service registration McDonald's Corporation.

A lit-tle break from it all,   Is the break that you need.

Slower

You de- serve a break to-day,   So get up and get a- way   to Mc-

Don-ald's,   So get up   and   get a - way   to Mc-

You Get A Lot To Like With A Marlboro

Verse

The bet-ter the ma-kin's, the bet-ter the smoke, You get bet-ter ma-kin's in a Marl-boro, You're smok-ing bet-ter, when-ev-er you smoke, a Marl-boro Cig-ar-

Permission to reproduce granted by Philip Morris Incorporated

You, You're The One ™

Words by Keith Reinhard &
Dan Nichols
Music by Ginny Redington

Copyright 1975 by G & W Publishing Corp. c/o Publishers' Licensing Corporation, 488 Madison Ave., NY, NY 10022. All rights reserved. Used by permission.
Permission to reproduce granted by McDonald's Corporation.
TM - Service mark owned by McDonald's Corporation.

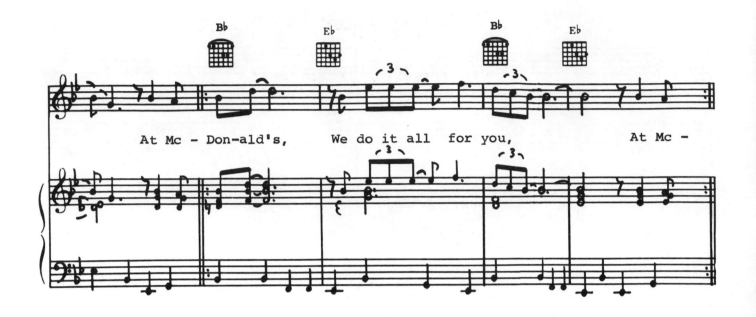

At Mc - Don-ald's,   We do it all for you,   At Mc -

You'll Wonder Where
The Yellow Went

Pepsodent TOOTHPASTE

Moderato

You'll won - der where the yel - low went, when you brush your teeth with Pep - so - dent!

Registered trademark of Lever Brothers Company

You've Come A Long Way Baby

VIRGINIA SLIMS

Moderato

Lyrics:

You've come a long way, Ba - by, to get where you got to to-day, You've got Vir - gin - ia Slims now, Ba - by, You've come a long, long way.

Permission to reproduce granted by Philip Morris Incorporated

Yum, Yum, Bumble Bee

Moderato

Yum, yum, Bum-ble Bee, Bum-ble Bee Tu-na, I love Bum-ble Bee, Bum-ble Bee Tu-na, Yum, yum, Bum-ble Bee, Bum-ble Bee tu-na, I love a sand-wich made with Bum-ble Bee.

Bum-ble Bee! The best tu-na in the sea, is the

tu - na we call, Yum, yum, Bum-ble Bee, Bum - ble Bee tu - na.

Copyright 1972 by Rising Sun Music, Inc.

IDs

Lestoil

Moderato

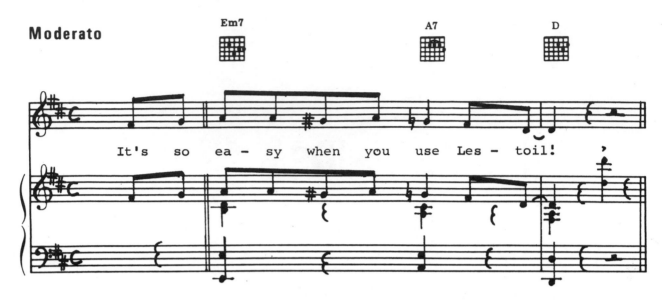

It's so ea-sy when you use Les-toil!

Permission to reproduce granted by Noxell Corporation

N-E-S-T-L-É-'S

Moderato

N - E - S - T - L - É - S, Nest-lé's makes the ve-ry best choc-'late.

A trademark of the Nestle''s Company, Inc.

Now A Word

From Our Sponsor...

The New York Times
(Home Delivery)

Words by Paula Green
Music by Tommy Goodman

sit around regretfully without it?   Unthinkable! Must you miss the latest

talk about a play?   Must you only hear what others say about it?   Im-

possible!   Good heavens, Sir or Madam, call today!

(Sung)

Eight

hun-dred, three, two, five, six, four hun-dred,   that's the

splen-did toll-free num-ber that you phone, Eight hun-dred, three, two

five, six, four hun-dred, (Spoken) And say, "By George, I want The

New York Times at home!"

Copyright 1975 by The New York Times
Permission to reproduce granted by Green Dolmatch Inc.

Index

E

F

G

H

I

J